MY MILITARY SERVICE
DURING
WORLD WAR II

Edward G. Hardy

My Military Service During World War II

© 2012 Eward G. Hardy

ISBN: 978-1-61170-104-3

Published by:

 Robertson Publishing™
www.RobertsonPublishing.com

Printed in the USA and UK on acid-free paper.
To purchase additional copies of this book go to:

amazon.com
barnesandnoble.com
www.rp–author.com/hardy

TABLE OF CONTENTS

INTRODUCTION

My story takes place during the trying years of World War II. I decided to place my memoirs in type. I thought my family might find it interesting to read about my life as it was during another time. There were parts of my life the family may not be familiar with and this memoir will help fill in those gaps.

I have written candidly and described my life the way it really was and I have tried to include the tears as well as the laughter. This is not an encyclopedic collection of everything but rather a selection of remembrances that highlighted my life. These are episodes that I hope the family will find informative as well as interesting.

I am writing this memoir in 1998, fifty-seven years after World War II. I feel I can now reflect on my life with greater serenity and objectivity than at any other time.

Camaraderie in wartime service can never be fully explained to persons who have not lived that experience. You get to know your fellow soldiers probably better than anyone in your previous life. It is the closeness of your situation that leads to the comradeship.

You live together, sleep together, and train together. You work and fight together. You depend upon one another for your very being. You suffer together and sometimes die together. What affects your buddy's life affects yours as well. This camaraderie is greatly manifested once you arrive overseas. You only know your buddies. The bond grows much stronger.

The ties that grow between men who live, on occasion, savagely together, relentlessly communing with death, are ties of great strength. There is a sense of fidelity to each other in a corps of men who have endured so long and whose hope in the end can be so small.

Chapter One

BASIC TRAINING

I enlisted in the army on April 2, 1942, in Elkhart, Indiana at the age of twenty. This was four months after the Japanese had attacked Pearl Harbor. I was sent to Toledo, Ohio for a physical examination. We were then inducted into the army, placed on a train and shipped to Fort Benjamin Harrison, Indiana. We were issued army clothing and garrisoned in tents. We spent three days there, then were shipped to Jefferson Barracks outside of St. Louis, Missouri. On April 5, I mailed my civilian clothing home. During the war, military personnel were not allowed to wear civilian clothing.

There were about 30,000 troops at Jefferson Barracks. I was assigned to Flight C, the 27th Technical School Squadron. We bunked in tents and later moved into barracks.

At Jefferson Barracks we received a small pox vaccination and many other shots including typhoid, tetanus, cholera, etc.

We learned the "Articles of War" and close order drilling. We were given gas masks and Tommy guns. Basic training was extremely difficult for me. We trained for war. We attended many lectures and pulled our share of K.P. When selected for K.P., you would place a towel on the foot of your bunk. You were then awakened at 3:00 AM. After reporting to the kitchen you usually worked until 8:00 or 9:00 PM.

While at J. B., ten of us were selected as "Soldiers of the Week". We were honor guards for visiting Hollywood stars. They were appearing at a local St. Louis theater to raise money for war bonds. The show was called "The Hollywood Cavalcade". The stars traveled around the country putting on their show. My job was to open their limousine door and help them any way that I could. Some of those stars were: Bob Hope, Ann Sheridan, Constance Bennett, Francis Langford, and Jerry Colonna, just to mention a few.

Teaching us to become soldiers was no easy task. We were taught to follow orders without question. There was the right way and the Army way. We continually policed our quarters. Cigarette smokers were taught to rip the paper from the tobacco, then roll the paper into little round balls prior to scattering them. After a few days into our training we were issued wooden guns. They were the same length as the Springfield rifle, with a bayonet attached. We would fall in by our barracks and march to the drill field. We learned the manual of arms with those rifles.

After practicing for two weeks with the wooden guns we were issued one Springfield rifle for every two men in line. One man carried the gun to drill field, where turns were taken in manual of arms and bayonet practice. Another person would carry the rifle back to the supply headquarters at the end of the day.

We learned to field strip the Springfield rifle, the Colt 45 handgun and the Thompson machine gun. The greater part of the day was spent on the drill field. We also attended lectures and went on ten-mile hikes with full field packs. On two occasions we practiced on the rifle range.

We usually had the evenings free. The first week of training was very exhausting. We sometimes fell asleep right after the evening meal and did not wake until the next morning. We attended camp shows on occasion at the tent city. Hollywood stars and big name bands made their appearance.

We would fall out for retreat on Mondays and Fridays. We wore our dress uniforms on those occasions. We would fall out in front of our barracks or tents at 2:00 PM to get in formation. We would not pass in review until 5:30 PM. It was very tiring, especially after being on the drill field all morning. I got sick in rank on one occasion but the corporal in charge would not let me fall out of formation. Marching that day was a real chore.

Drilling in the cold Missouri rain was not uncommon. It was not unusual to pull extra duty in the evening for a miner infraction of a rule or an order. One time an officer came into our barracks and we failed to call attention. Because of that, we had to mop the barracks floor with toothbrushes. We received no leave that evening.

On May 11, 1942, we said "Goodbye" to Jefferson Barracks, the number one U.S. Concentration Camp, we thought. We boarded a train for Charleston, South Carolina. We were going overseas. Wearing our winter O.D.s, we carried an A bag and a B bag. The A bag contained clothing and articles needed while on board the ship. Everything in the B bag would be placed in the hold of the ship. In addition to the two bags, we carried a full field pack that contained a pup tent, one blanket and our steel helmet. Hung from our shoulders were a Tommy gun and a gas mask. Finally, we felt like soldiers and looked forward to whatever lay ahead. We had no idea where we were going but we were on our way.

Chapter Two

ACROSS THE ATLANTIC

Arriving at our destination on the outskirts of Charleston, we were assigned to barracks. We pulled no duties while in Charleston. We prepared for our overseas trip. We visited the P.X. and purchased last minute items. I wrote my last letter to my mother. We could not tell friends and family members where we were or where we were going. All correspondence for the next two and one half years was to be censored by the army.

Letter to Mother

I can't say a thing. The war is to blame.

Just write that I'm well and send my name.

I can't tell where I am. Can't mention the date.

I can't even mention the meals I ate.

Can't say where I'm going. Don't know where I will land.

Can't even inform you just how I stand.

Can't mention the wind. Not even the rain.

All Army maneuvers must secret remain.

Can't use a flashlight to guide myself at night.

Can't smoke a cigarette, except out of sight.

Can't keep a diary, for such is a sin.

Can't even keep the envelopes your letters come in.

Can't say for sure these words that I write

Will be passed by the censor

So I will just say, "Good night!"

A dirt road ran by our camp and we would take leisurely walks and talk to the local farmers along the way. Many farmers were black. I had never seen a black farmer up north. They seemed eager to converse with us. I was able to talk with several southern girls working at our P.X. They were interested in discussing job opportunities in the north.

We received more overseas shots. The shots made some men sick. One fellow would pass out whenever he received any shot. We also had several RAF pilots at this camp. They had been training in American fighter planes.

On May 26, 1942, our commanding officer, 1st Lieutenant Jarvis, called us together. He explained how we would board the troop ship the next day. He said we were now soldiers and he was proud of us. We would be the first Americans to arrive at our destination in World War II. That destination would remain nameless until we were at sea. A slip of the lip could sink a ship. He explained that we were expendable, but to keep our chins up for some of us would be coming home some day. How we conducted ourselves now could make a difference to those who would follow in the future. Our morale began to sag a little at that point.

He restricted us to our barracks that night.

On May 27, 1942, we ate a large breakfast, loaded the previously mentioned equipment on GMC trucks and were driven to the Charleston port of embarkation. We unloaded the trucks near a large warehouse and, with the equipment, waited to board the ship. (I might add that none of us had received any pay in the army up to that time).

We stood at ease with our pack, gas mask, our A and B bags, Tommy gun, and other miscellaneous equipment for about nine hours. This was without food or water. We could not leave the ranks. During this time it began to rain. It came blowing down around the buildings in slanting sheets. We were soon wet to the skin. The rain continued intermittently throughout the day. We felt like, and looked like, miserable wet rats as we finally boarded the ship that night. The ship was the Santa Paula of the Grace Lines. We did not realize it but this was to be our home for the next sixty days.

We were given no directions where to go after climbing the gangplank. I struggled with my equipment until I found a stateroom. Dumping everything on the floor, I climbed in a bunk and was soon sound asleep. The time was 12:30 AM May 26, 1942. It had been an extremely long day. I was hungry, wet, and angry at the world.

On the morning of May 28, very early, we pulled away from the dock and headed out to sea. The sun was just beginning to throw its warm light on the city of Charleston. At that hour it seemed like everyone was still sleeping. I stood by the railing watching the land slowly sink from view. I cannot describe the feeling that came over me, steaming out into that dark sub infested Atlantic, having no idea where we were going or if we would ever return. It was the loneliest feeling of my young life.

While standing in the chow line that first day at sea, it suddenly hit home as to what we were going to be up against. We were given orders on how we were to conduct ourselves while on board. We were assigned quarters for the duration of our voyage. Fifteen of us were assigned to the ship library where hammocks had been provided. We were issued meal tickets. The color of the ticket indicated what time you were to eat. I was to eat at 6:30 AM and 5:30 PM.

The ship was blacked out from dusk until sun up. No lights on deck after dark were allowed. There would be no smoking on deck after dark. Any man caught making a light at night could have been shot.

The SS Santa Paula was a civilian passenger ship. The

ship was five hundred and eight feet long. She was seventy-two feet wide. She had a depth of forty-eight feet. Se had a displacement tonnage of sixteen thousand, six hundred and seventy-six tons. Her gross tonnage was nine thousand, one hundred and thirty-nine. The ship's letters were AKEA. The engines were steam turbines. The horsepower was twelve thousand. Her speed was nineteen knots. The ship was registered out of San Francisco. Her official number was 232,003. The ship had a capacity of one hundred tons of salt water. The swimming pool was thirty-five feet by twenty feet. The pool had been converted into a latrine when she began transporting troops.

Our fist stop was at the harbor of Bermuda. This was on the 30th of May. The troops were not allowed to go ashore while in Bermuda. We lay at anchor while our convoy was formed. Sailboats came out to greet us. Those on board yelled in encouragement. Leaving Bermuda, we avoided land mines placed in the harbor entrance by our Allies.

We were joined in the convoy by fellow troopships, the Mariposa of the Matson Line, the Marmacs and the British ship Chateau Thierry. Naval vessels included the battleship Texas, destroyers Dallas, Ludlow, Barnard, and the Cole. The convoy now consisted of thirty-one ships.

My only duty was that of fireguard. I checked certain sections of the ship for fires and keept a lookout for any problems among the troops. I carried my Tommy gun. I had to remain on deck and make certain there were no lights on deck after sun down.

Life on board was very monotonous. Fresh water was used for drinking and cooking. The soap issued to us did not lather in the salt water. There was no way to keep yourself clean. We did have a nice trick to clean our clothing. Tying our clothing with a piece of rope, we would play out the line from the stern. The clothing would skip and turn in the ship's wake. Twenty minutes later the clothing, providing it was still on the line, would be pulled in cleaned. We would lay the clothing in the sun to dry. Many a trooper lost their clothing in this manner.

On occasion, while looking out over the ocean, you would see what you thought was a submarine. Everyone would begin yelling and running for cover. The sub usually turned out to be a whale cruising along among the ships. They would dart to the front several times until tiring of the game, then swim from view.

Flying fish would be seen daily. They would leap out of the water and fly into one another. We saw a few sharks. Porpoises would race along the side in small schools.

Our hammocks were made from pieces of steel rod. Three-by-six foot canvas was stretched between the rails. They could be folded up during the day to allow passage in the aisle. They were hung about one foot from the floor to the height of the ceiling. Hammocks were installed in every available space. In some quarters there were installed at least ten feet high. The hammock was your sleeping and storage area. My personal items were stuffed into the bag and used for a pillow. At night, during the rough weather, the ship would roll and some fellows were tossed to the floor.

The PX was not opened until several days out to sea. It was then open only every other day. You could purchase one pack of cigarettes and one Hershey bar – nothing else. This was our first case of rationing. We received a partial paycheck of $15.99. This was my first paycheck since joining the service. My first full months pay was in foreign currency. My fifteen dollars did not last long. Gambling was one method of getting rid of it. Card and dice games were ever present. Having no idea where we were going, the thought of losing my money was never a serious problem. Stateside, a privates monthly pay at that time was only $21.00 per month. Overseas you received an additional $10.00. Our pay was increased in 1942.

We called the Santa Paula the slave ship. The only thing lacking was the chains. Conditions were deplorable. The food was extremely bad. I had previously lost the top half of my mess kit and subsequently had to eat out of the bottom portion. The KPs would dump the food into my mess kit. Presenting the bottom portion of my kit, they would slop hominy grits, canned milk and add two prunes. This all ran together in a gooey mess. This would round out my average breakfast.

At the evening meal, we had the choice of tea or coffee. We could have no seconds. No milk or water was available. After receiving your food, you looked for a place to eat. We had to stand while eating. Tables were approximately twenty feet long, three-and-one-half feet wide, and four-and-one-half feet high. A four-inch rail ran around the top edge of the table. At first I had no understanding why the edge was raised – I soon found the reason. During rough weather the ship would roll with the waves. Mess kits not held down would slide off the table. Many times even with that rail, during extremely rough weather, the floor would be littered with food. Garbage cans placed at the end of each table would overturn. Their contents slopped back and forth across one's feet.

Tables

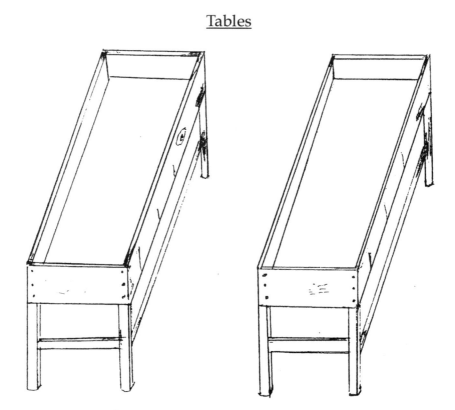

Another misery was the fact we had to wear old cork vested life preservers. They were dirty, and stained from many years of use. When you squeezed between the men standing at the table in order to reach a vacant eating spot, you would involuntarily rub against the back of every man between you and your objective. At times you would bump a person and they would jamb a fork or spoon into your face. They would grumble or cuss you out.

Men would throw their life jackets overboard just to observe if they would float. Many disappeared under the water. They would not have been of much help should the necessity of their use arrive.

Evening meals consisted of Spam, a boiled egg and an apple. The eggs were rubbery and grayish in color. Most of us stopped eating them after a few days. We were always

hungry when leaving the mess hall. Troops suffered from being hungry and having diarrhea or sickness.

Officers had their mess hall at the end of ours in a private
little room. They were seated at tables and were served by
waiters. Bowls of fruit were placed on their tables. Watching the officers eating so well made us feel like second-class
citizens. We would have fought for the food they threw away.
One of the enlisted men said he bought a sandwich from an officer for $5.00. Back in the States $5.00 would have purchased
two complete meals at that time. Standing by the railing in
the evening, watching discarded food from the officer's mess
being dumped into the sea brought many angry comments
from enlisted men.

We had a public address system on board. News about the
war was broadcast daily. Newsworthy stories aboard the ship
were also announced.

Thomas Thornton, a close friend, was sick when we boarded the ship in Charleston. The doctor who was examining
him thought he was faking and ordered him aboard. After
two days at sea Tom died. He was buried in Freetown, West
Africa, upon our arrival there.

We spent our time playing cards, reading, shooting crap,
and drilling to stay in shape. Boxing matches were held
among the troops. During the day, the weather was usually
warm and we spent most of the day outdoors.

Rumors concerning our destination were rampant. Many
fellows, afraid of being caught below deck during an attack
would stay our on deck during the night. In the evening, I
would lie on the deck, my head resting against the main mast.
I would gaze at the stars while the mast moved back and forth
across the sky. Sometimes I would fall asleep in that position.

The ship swimming pool had been converted into a latrine.

The top was covered with boards and a tarpaulin. We used the top as a recreational area. Steps led to the pool's bottom. An MP sat near the bottom issuing two squares of toilet tissue per man. We were told to use both sides. Approximately ten urinals lined one wall. There were about four rows of stools. Stools were placed back to back.

Stools

Most of us suffered from diarrhea and/or dysentery. Sea-sickness was common. You would observe a fellow suffering from both seasickness and diarrhea, using two stools – one for his diarrhea and the other for vomiting. Stools would plug up and overflow. Usually about half of the stools were not operational. The floor was covered with wooden slats, and was constantly wet. While setting there in deep concentration, the ship would roll from side to side. Your by-product would rise on each roll and pat you on the fanny. No sir, two pieces of toilet paper were not enough!

Threats of German submarines were common. You never grew accustomed to the anxiety of the situation that you found yourself in. You would try to place it in the back of you mind. During our May crossing of the Atlantic, the activities of the German wolf packs were at their height. Many allied ships were sunk along our eastern coast. Navy gunners aboard our ship would practice their gunnery, shooting over the waves with their "pompom". They were guns mounted on platforms on which the gunner sat and fired using both hands. I never knew the proper name of those guns. We called them "pompoms" because of the noise they made. As I recall, there were four guns on board.

Chapter Three

AFRICA

Friday, June 12, 1942 the convoy arrived in Freetown, West Africa. A submarine net stretched across the harbor entrance. A steamer lay sunk on our port side, with its mast and bow sticking out of the water, a victim of the war. The submarine netting was closed behind us as we entered the harbor. I counted around two hundred ships laying at anchor in the harbor. They were mostly Free French and some English vessels.

Freetown appeared beautiful from the harbor. Palm trees lined the entire coast, and there were many white houses with red tile roofs. We were not allowed to go ashore. Our dead friend, Tom Thorton, was the only enlisted man allowed ashore. He was buried somewhere in Freetown. The night of Tom's burial, the officers threw a dance party for the nurses on their upper deck. This obstinate and uncaring action, on their part, was the straw that broke the camel's back. The troops became rebellious and started throwing rotten fruit at the officers. One must remember the troops were dirty and hungry. They were sick from diarrhea and/or seasickness. We realized that if the officers did not respect the burial of our friend, they certainly had no compassion for our plight.

The music stopped. Two officers came over to the railing above us and began berating the troops. We were insubordinate and mutinous. My CO, 2nd LT. Jarvis, was hit in the face with a rotten apple. When things quieted down we were allowed to explain our position. The officers apologized and postponed their dance. I thought there would be repercussions from Lt. Jarvis. However, nothing occurred over the matter and everything was soon back to normal.

On our second night in Freetown an exceedingly powerful

storm swept in from the sea. Clothing, laid out to dry, was blown into the sea. We stripped and stood in the drenching rain. This was our first fresh water bath since leaving the States.

The weather remained extremely hot in Freetown. It was June 19th. Because the Germans had taken Dakar, which was only 400 miles from Freetown, the convoy headed south along the African West coast.

There were thirty-five ships at that time in our convoy. The convoy included two British battleships and four cruisers. We fired at an Italian airplane but he flew away unharmed. Several times during our trip, depth bombs were deployed. We were never told why they were dropped or the result of their action. The British were in charge of our convoy once we left Freetown. Running alongside us were the British cruisers, the Rodney and the Nelson.

I made friends with Johnny Mooney from London. He was in the barrage balloon battalion. He explained the balloons were fastened with rope or steel cable. They would float at a certain height and sometimes supported a net. The balloons were used to force enemy aircraft to maintain altitudes too high for accurate bombing. Their fabric was self-sealing when punctured by bullets. I lost track of Johnny when we arrived at our destination.

By this time, I had been at sea longer than on land while in the service. During our sojourn on the Santa Paula, we lost two men overboard. A search of the ship was made but they were never found. We had been told previously, the ship would not turn around for a recovery should one of us fall overboard. Such action, if taken, could have jeopardized the lives of all the troops.

During rough weather, it was difficult to keep your footing. The sea crashed against the side and spray blew across the deck. Objects not secured slid from side to side. Sounds of falling objects were heard throughout the ship. The old vessel creaked and moaned in the heavy sea.

We arrived in Durban, South Africa on July 4th. Rounding the Cape of Good Hope prior to arriving in Durban would be another story in itself. After the docking procedure was accomplished, we stood at the railings and threw coins to the native divers. Some of the divers would climb the anchor ropes. Durban seemed like a beautiful city. Behind the city, lying along the waterfront, stretched hills covered with palm trees and well kept homes. A park lay in the very center of the city.

The ship lay at the dock for two days. Half the ships compliment was allowed shore leave the first day. I went ashore the second day. I walked into town from the dock. Walking on solid ground created some problems. My legs weren't used to the solid ground.

Black men wearing shorts and American Indian type headdresses were lined up at the gangplank with their rickshaws (jinrikisha). I learned this was a time-honored method of transportation in this part of the world. The rickshaw was a small two-wheeled hooded carriage, pulled by one man. It was my understanding that rickshaw man's life was shortened because he spent his life running most of the day. I refused the ride and walked into Durban.

We were the first American Forces to arrive in Durban during World War II. At first the people thought we were Australians. One woman asked if I was a Yank, I responded in the affirmative. That was the first time I had been called a Yank. I noticed there were few young men in the town. I understood this was due to their being in the service of their country.

Having gone without a good meal since leaving the States, I began checking every restaurant for an opportunity to enjoy a decent meal. Every restaurant had a large line of British and American troops extending down the sidewalk. Wanting to get away from fellow soldiers and be by myself for a little while, I climbed on a train. The young lady conductor said I could ride to the end of the line at the extreme edge of the city. I was surprised to see this lady in charge of the train. It was due, of course, to the young men leaving for the service. One must remember that during this period of our history, most women were not performing that kind of work. The role of women in those days was to marry and raise their children. The man supported the family. During the war years, it became necessary for women to play a very active part in the war effort. They filled vacancies created by the men leaving for military service. They did a fantastic job regardless of the job they were required to fill.

Hearing me talk to the conductor, the occupants of the train gathered around asking questions concerning the United States. They were most anxious to converse with an American and get our views concerning the war, etc. For many people, this was their first opportunity. Our conversations were very interesting.

Arriving at the end of the line, I descended and strolled around the area. I had only thirty minutes before the tram would leave for my return into town. While talking to two English soldiers an elderly English civilian walked over to us from his home. He invited us to join him for tea. I had to refuse because of my tight schedule.

Walking down to the edge of a nearby hill I looked over into the jungle. A small village lay before me. It was a typical African compound of around twenty-five thatched huts that all looked alike. They were made of sun-dried mud. The roofs seemed to be made of branches of palm or banana leaves. The huts were round and about twenty feet in diameter. There was not a blade of grass in the compound. Hundreds of bare feet had worn the grass down until nothing but hard packed earth remained. I felt lost in time. The village so starkly represented everything I had read about Africa. Lost in my thoughts, I boarded the train and soon was deposited in the center of Durban.

Once back in town I spent my last few minutes walking around trying to absorb the strange sights. Not being used to all the exercise, I started experiencing cramps in my stomach. I began looking for a bathroom. I found a public toilet, but there was a long line of troops waiting. I fell into the line waiting my turn. A conversation was struck with an English soldier who had been in the battle of London. London had been bombed for seventy-nine days and nights. Not being able to sweat the line any longer, I began searching for an alternative.

I ran down an alley and turned into a courtyard. It was full of Zulus conducting a ceremonial dance. Although it was extremely interesting, I could not linger. Hurrying along the alley I saw a sign indicating they sold petrol. Knowing this meant gasoline, I asked the attendant if I could use his toilet. He did not understand. When I changed it to "may I use your latrine", he understood. Never have I felt so totally relieved. Here I was in a strange country, having to go to the toilet and not finding a place to relieve myself.

I returned to the Santa Paula and we continued our journey.

Chapter Four

FROM AFRICA TO INDIA

We had been aboard the Santa Paula for fifty-two days and were heading for India. It was July 1942 and the troop ship contained several thousand American servicemen and women. There were also several English troops. The Santa Paula was a luxury liner now pressed into service for the military as a troop ship.

Fresh water was saved for drinking. Showers were taken out in the open on the lower deck. We had been issued ordinary soap, which did not lather in salt water. We had to rub the dirt from our bodies. Subsequently, I had developed two large abscesses in the pit of my arm. While bathing, you could see army nurses and officers watching from their upper deck. They had showers in their staterooms. Some of the enlisted men would not bathe when the nurses were present.

I had reported on sick call at the ship's medical dispensary for treatment. The doctor had me lay on a table in order to make an examination. Blood rushed from my right armpit, ran under my side and collected in a widening pool under my back. Lancing the boil had been excruciating. The army doctor held the bloody scalpel before my eyes;

"Well, we got one of them," he said. Having one abscess lanced, he was preparing to lance the second. Just at that moment, the protecting destroyer escorts began blowing their whistles indicating an alert.

Everyone present ran to the porthole and looked out. I heard them say the navy was laying a smoke screen around our convoy. I lay there awaiting the doctor's return, knowing the other abscess had to be lanced. That particular smoke screen was unfounded. The ocean liner Queen Mary had crossed our convoy heading for America. I believe the Queen Mary was the only liner to travel without a convoy during the war.

The doctor's continued their operations without the benefit of an anesthetic. I was placed in the ship's hospital where I remained until we reached Karachi, India.

We did not know what to expect on our arrival there. We headed north into the Mozambique straits, passing the island of Madagascar. The English were fighting to take the island from the French. The fighting was sporadic. The British corvettes had joined our convoy: the Rock, the Rose, and the Violet. They had provided us with fine escort duty. The Mariposa and the Santa Paula left the protection of the convoy and headed unescorted for Karachi. Now running without the protection of the British corvettes, we raced toward Karachi.

Our run up the east coast of Africa was uneventful with the exception of the unexpected appearance of an armed merchantman. They caused us some worry and confusion for a while.

We were very fortunate in that we never lost a ship in our convoy. Many times depth charges rocked our ship but there was no damage to any of the ships.

We arrived in Karachi on the fifty-eighth day of our voyage. Every thing seemed very strange; the natives with their turbans, the odd-looking buildings, cattle roaming the streets and walking in and out of the stores, etc. We disembarked on the 25th of July. Another soldier helped me carry my equipment ashore. We were loaded onto army trucks and driven through the city of Karachi. We were taken about fifteen miles into the barren countryside. Malair Field would be our temporary home for two weeks.

We were assigned to barracks that were made of mortar and stone. Every twenty feet a wall divided the barracks. Into these "bays" were assigned eight men per bay. We were given Indian beds to sleep on. We received one mattress, two blankets, and one mosquito netting (a mosquito bar). The bunks were wooden, framed with hemp rope stretched lengthwise and crosswise.

A "T" frame was placed at the head and foot of the bunk. Over the "T" frame was placed your mosquito bar. You had to sleep under the mosquito bar because the anopheles mosquito carried malaria and yellow fever.

Mosquito Bar

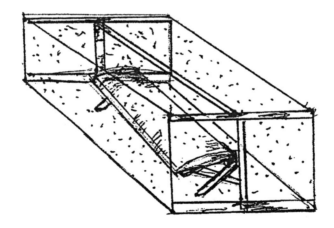

The bunks were very hard. Being young, we soon grew accustomed to them. My bunk was my living quarters for two and one half years.

Equipment was stored around our bunks. Letters to loved ones were written there. There were no tables upon which to write. Bunks were used for informal activities such as playing cards, shooting caps, etc.

On our first night in India, Jimmy Jackson (who was from Kentucky) and I went into the surrounding area to hunt snakes. The arid desert contained a lot of cactus and there were numerous arroyos running in all directions. It was a foreboding area. Using our flashlights we found several different varieties of snakes. The night had cooled off from the blazing sun and the night animals were out to collect their evening meals. We killed several snakes but allowed most of them to escape. One six-foot cobra was taken back to camp. It was the only snake we really recognized. Our friends thought we were crazy.

Leaving Malair we were transferred to Karachi Air Force Base, the 51st Headquarters Squadron. At Karachi we pulled guard duty and lived in World War II tents. We slept on army cots without the benefit of a mattress. The tents had no flooring and small animals made their home there. They would pop out of their holes on any occasion. We grew accustomed to knocking our shoes against something before putting them on. Some lizards grew up to several feet long and presented quite a problem.

When you pulled gate guard you wore a Colt 45 on your web belt. You had to check every person entering and leaving the camp. We guarded payrolls and important people. I once guarded Generalissimo Chang Kai Shek and Madam Chang Kai Shek. We guarded against clandestine operations.

When I walked the perimeter I carried a Tommy gun. Guard duty hours varied; two hours on and four hours off. This was seven days a week. We then went to four hours on and eight hours off duty. Walking the perimeter post at 2:00AM or 3:00AM was lonely and eerie. Different animal sounds would keep you alert. We were more frightened of snakes and unknown animals than we were of saboteurs and spies. After walking post for a brief time, your eyes grew accustomed to the darkness.

One evening our commanding officer burst into our tent

and ordered us to grab our weapons and follow him. He drove us to an Indian tent located on the base. Indian merchants were allowed to set up their tents in certain areas and sell merchandise to the soldiers. The officer ordered two fellows to guard the front and rear of the large tent. He and I went into the tent. I held those present under guard with my Tommy gun. He yelled, "You son of a b....! You are a God D.... spy!" The headman was placed under arrest. We searched the tent and found a wireless radio in the back room hidden under clothing. He had been sending messages to the Japs from our very base. Ironically, just two days prior to this, I had taken this same person into town for a good meal. I thought him to be a nice fellow.

On one occasion I was assigned to a garbage detail. Having no knowledge of that duty, I was a little befuddled by the assignment. I rode the garbage truck to the dump area. Several dozen Indians met us. They immediately began climbing into the truck and clutching food. I had to beat them off so we could unload. I did not enjoy this job. In 1942 there was a great famine thousands of Indians died that year from starvation. In Karachi we saw people dying on the streets and sidewalks.

Our tents were located at the end of the runway. Planes took off and landed over our heads. On two occasions P-40 airplanes flew into tents. One plane crashed and burned just twenty feet from our tent. A second plane came in too low and pulled the tent right off its foundation. A record was playing at the time and it kept right on playing. Luckily, when the planes hit most of the fellows were out.

In town beggars constantly pestered us. They deformed their children in order to ply on ones sympathy. They were among the untouchable class. Shoeshine boys would spit beetle juice on our shoes and then want to shine them clean. If you gave one child a coin you would soon have a dozen children following you, begging. Mothers would hold their child up to you and say, "Buckshee Sob. No mama. No papa." They had nothing to eat and were destitute. Indians by the hundreds slept on the sidewalks. It seemed that thousands had no homes and just wandered the streets.

Pretty young untouchable girls would follow the cattle throughout the city. When the cattle had excrement the girls would give you a big smile as they swept it into their baskets. Later it would be plastered on the side of their home to dry and then be used in the winter to heat their home.

Chapter Five

A NEW CAREER

In October 1943, thirty of us fellows were transferred to Landhi Field. Landhi was an airfield just a few miles from the town of Karachi. Landhi was on the southeastern edge of the Sind Desert. It was home to a pursuit fighter group called the FRTU (Fighter Replacement Training Unit). Our duties were to train pilots in combat tactics. These were new pilots arriving from the States. I was trained as a mechanic and as a crew chief. I earned two MOS letters. Those letters represented your military qualifications and job duties. We worked on the P-40. As the war progressed we were given newer planes, the P-51 and the P-47. Later, back in the States, I worked on the P-38; the Lightning.

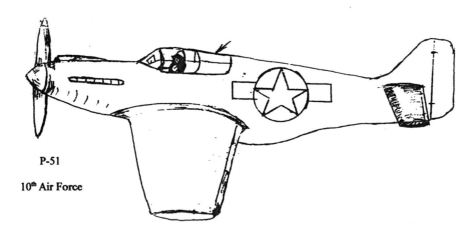

P-51

10ᵗʰ Air Force

As a crew chief, we were assigned two planes per man. Our responsibilities were to maintain, service, and keep the planes flying. Our average day would begin at sunrise. We pre-checked the engines at various speeds. Once we were assured the engine was functioning properly, we would walk around the plane checking all movable parts. If the preflight check proved satisfactory we then checked the oil and filled the gas tanks with one hundred octane gas. The armament crew serviced the machine guns. If the mission called for bombing a machine gun would be placed under the plane's belly.

I had an incident concerning a West Point Major who reported to my plane for an early morning mission. When he was seated in the cockpit we strapped on his seat belt and shoulder straps. He was new to the P-40, so I had to give him a complete checkout. I explained the bomb release lever beside his seat. He thought it was too low and proceeded to tie his handkerchief to the lever. He thought this would make it easier for him to release the bomb. In doing so, he did release the bomb. I heard it hit the cement abutment below the plane. I told him to release his seat belt and I jumped off the wing and began running yelling "live bomb!" We ran through the preflight line, dove into a slit trench and there for about five minutes. The bomb failed to explode. We walked rather sheepishly back to the plane and the Major completed his mission without further incident.

Major work on planes was accomplished about one mile from our preflight line. When it became necessary to make extensive repairs, we would taxi the plane to that area. I enjoyed this very much. I would speed up the engine, release the brakes, and speed down the preflight line. On occasion the tail would rise from the ground. I found this exhilarating.

We pulled a twenty-hour inspection on the planes. We also pulled a fifty-hour and a one-hundred-hour inspection. Each inspection was more detailed than the previous one. An inspector would check your work. Any plane that failed to pass inspection was grounded.

During a mission the ground crew at Landhi would gather in the Crew Chief shack. There we would sweat out the return of the pilots and our planes. We never really knew the pilots. Once they were trained they moved to other bases.

The planes were parked out in the open and we worked on them there, regardless of the weather. However, it only rained about twice a year in the desert. Most days were very hot. Many days the temperature was well over one hundred degrees. Winter nights were chilly. We had to use an extra blanket because we had no heat in our quarters.

To clean our fatigues we would soak them in gasoline for the day. By the evening they would be nice and clean and were then hung over cactus to dry.

We averaged around two plane crashes a week. Many men were lost throughout the year. Most of those lost were pilots. They were unaccustomed to the plane in which they were training. Occasionally a pilot, making an approach to the field, would bank too steeply and wing into the ground. In most cases the gas tank would explode and the plane would burn. Fire trucks, we called them "Meat Wagons", would rush to the scene, but were usually too late. We crew chiefs would run to the scene and attempt to rescue the pilot but many times we could do nothing except watch him burn. It was horrifying to stand by helplessly and watch a trapped man screaming while he was being cremated alive. The remains would usually be removed the next day after the fire cooled down. We grew accustomed to violent deaths but never to the smell of burning flesh.

We lost many planes. I recall a flight of six planes taking off on a mission. Two of those were planes I crewed. The flight leader was the only one who returned from the mission.

Preflight crews from our field were seldom briefed on the results of a mission. If your plane did not return you were eventually assigned another. We usually had more pilots than planes.

I passed the mental examination for Aviation Cadet Training. While waiting to return to the States for this training some of the pilots would let me go aloft with them in a trainer plane (AT-6). Once in the air they would turn the controls over to me. I enjoyed this very much. It was an escape from the hot preflight line. One such day during a practice dogfight with a P-40 I began to get airsickness. I took off my hat and proceeded to fill it. The rolls and loops, as well as the diving, had been too much for me. I threw my hat away as we taxied back to the parking area.

A pilot approached me one morning and said he was going up in a P-51 for practice skip bombing and asked if I wanted to ride along. I jumped at the chance. The speed of the P-51 would be exhilarating. The radio equipment had been removed from the compartment behind the pilot and by pushing hard I could slide into this vacancy.

We took off in a hurry. The speed was terrific. As the pilot banked I would slide over to the down side of the canopy. I couldn't wear a parachute or buckle myself in for there wasn't enough room under the canopy. I just hung onto the pilot's headrest, slipping and sliding under the flexography canopy. He made a wide turn, then lined up with the target and came in very low to the ground. Cactus whizzed by the side of our plane. It reminded me of passing telephone poles at a high rate of speed.

Suddenly the plane lurched hard to the right. The pilot corrected it and released the bomb. Pulling up and away he made for the runway.

Looking back I saw the bomb hit the target dead center. After landing, I climbed out on the wing and noticed the right wing tip was gone. The cactus had sheared it clean off. We must have been about six feet off the ground when it happened. At around four hundred miles per hour, that was a little hairy. I then congratulated the pilot on his expertise.

My C.O. canceled my orders to return to the States for aviation cadet training. He explained that we had lost many officers in the invasion of North Africa. It was his feeling that I could possibly be transferred to officer's training school in order to replace an officer lost there. Transfers from one branch of the army to another were a possibility in those days.

Thus I never did fulfill my dream of becoming a pilot.

During the night camel caravans crossed the desert near our field. They traveled in a single file. The lead camel wore a bell around its neck. It was similar to a cowbell. You could hear them approaching and continue to hear them long after they had disappeared. They had a rhythmic ring about them. Sounds travel a long way in the desert.

During the night small desert jackals would approach the camp area. You would hear them crying throughout the night. Their sound was not unlike that of a baby crying. We caught one and carried it into the camp. It looked like an American red fox, but small like a cat.

There were a variety of snakes in the Sind desert. Cobras and Kraits were the most prevalent. During my thirty-one months in India, I knew of only one death due to snakebite. This fellow was gathering wood from the woodpile when a Krait struck him on the arm. He lived only a few minutes. It was a terrible death.

The cobras killed many Indians every year. The reason more Americans were not bitten was the attitude of the Indians and the GIs toward the Cobra. Indians regarded the Cobra as sacred, sometimes as the reincarnation of a God, and would not kill them. On the other hand, the Americans in CBI (China, Burma, and India) wiped out Cobras as fast as they appeared around our installations.

The caste of snake charmer gypsies would work only with the Cobra. The Cobra would throw itself into an upright position with its head extended. The snake charmer would gain the snakes attention by playing a flute and moving it rhythmically in front of the Cobra. The snake would sway back and forth with its movement. Occasionally, the snake charmer would release several snakes and allow the mongoose to fight them. The mongoose always won the battle.

The world's biggest snake was the Regal Python of Burma. It reached a length of thirty feet and weighed two hundred twenty-five pounds. The Indian python averaged around eighteen feet in length.

A Lester bag containing drinking water hung from a tripod in the sun near our quarters. The water was warm but never got real hot.

Snakes would congregate near our showers. The showers were originally built in the open. The ground was always damp around the area. Snakes would come out in the evening and lay on the cool damp ground. King Cobras would rise off the ground and stare at you in the face before striking. Some would spit venom at a person's eyes.

Upon rising in the morning the first thing you did was look for something crawling or sliding on the floor and in your shoes. Giant lizards loved to make dens in the shade of a tent. Centipedes were everywhere. You soon grew accustomed to knocking your shoes against something to clear them of anything that had crawled there during the night.

I recall two occasions when locusts made their appearance. Millions were in the air and on the ground. The sky was black with them. We tied handkerchiefs around our faces to keep them out of our eyes and mouth.

Locusts rested on everything and you had to continuously brush them from your body. Roads were greasy from crushed locusts and cars slid off the roads.

Sandstorms were major threats. Plans would be grounded. Those planes caught in the air during a sandstorm were in for a real rough time. Pilots would look for an alternate landing site. If they failed to locate a site they would have to take their chances on bailing out. During those storms the sand would get in your clothing, your food, and your personal belongings. We would cover our faces with handkerchiefs and wear sunglasses. It was extremely difficult to breathe. Your teeth grated against the sand in food. If possible, your best bet was to lay on your bunk and cover your head with a blanket.

Tongas were the normal method of transportation around the cities. It was a two wheeled cart pulled by a horse. Most of us would ride the Tongas or just walk around the bazaar. We walked among the crowds in the bazaar and looked for items to send home. The towns were always over-crowded. There were a few taxis that burned charcoal to run their engines. The main reason we went to town to get a decent meal at a restaurant. We usually attended a cinema. Most of the movies were English made. There were Indian movies but we could not understand them. Most American movies were rather old ones.

A friend and I managed to obtain weeklong passes. We got a ride on a C-47 bound for New Delhi. We waited in New Delhi for several hours before catching a ride to Agra, India. Our reason for going to Agra was to visit the Taj Mahal and take pictures for the fellows back at our field. Agra was the country's capital in 1503. The Taj sits on the back of the Jumna River. It dates back to about 3000BC and stands on the right bank of the Jumna about one mile from the old fort. This mausoleum is regarded as one of the wonders of the world.

Emperor Shahjahan erected it to the memory of his wife, the Empress Arjumand Ban Bagaum. They repose side by side. The Taj was made of white marble and red sandstone. Jewels and precious stones from various parts of India once were delicately inlaid both inside and outside the beautiful building. It was begun in 1631 and completed in 1648. They said about 20,000 laborers were employed. Some of the nearby buildings date back to about 250BC.

We walked behind the Taj to the Jumna River. A funeral pyre was taking place. The deceased lay on a carefully piled stack of wood. The fire had just been lit. The family stood by watching the body being consumed by the flames. A man and his little boy arrived. They proceeded to another location where we could see the remains of yet another pyre. They began scraping around in the cold ashes. Occasionally they would find a small bone. They would place every piece of bone, up to about two inches in length, in a small earthen jar.

We heard a funeral procession approaching. A family was coming to dispose of their dead. A young man held a baby wrapped in a brightly colored cloth. As we watched he threw the baby into the river. The brightly colored cloth floated away as the baby popped to the surface. A huge turtle rose from the turbid cloudy water. He grabbed the baby by the cheek of its fanny and disappeared into the depths. We noticed several large turtles heading in that direction.

Latrines and Showers

Our latrines and showers were built out in the open. They were built from airplane crates. (Planes were shipped to India and assembled in Karachi.) The latrines and showers were about one-hundred feet from our living quarters.

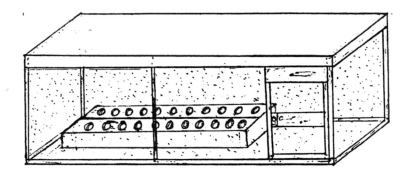

The latrines were screened against flying insects. There was no privacy from outside viewers.

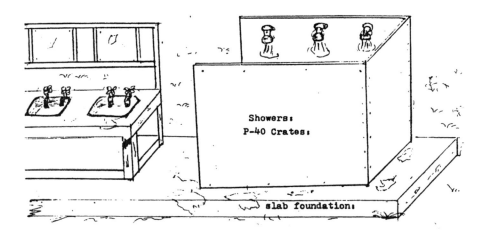

Chapter Six

THE HIMALAYAN MOUNTAINS

In 1943 several of us at Landhi Field were given leave for three weeks. The U.S. Government had made arrangements with the British for the use of a rest camp in the Himalayan Mountains. Troops were sent there for a little R. and R.

Six men occupied each compartment on the train trip. The seats were made of wooden slats and we slept on them at night. There was little room to get up and move about. Most of our food on the train was canned beef.

At Lahore station, during a short stop, we were ordered off the train. They began spraying cars with DDT. Hundreds of three-inch cockroaches began falling to the ground under the train. To think we had been sleeping with them running around was scary.

At every stop beggars, with fingers and parts of their bodies eaten away by leprosy, besieged us. Small dirty children cried, "No mama, no papa, no sister." Mothers carried babies on their hips. Sometimes they carried a jar or a basket on their heads. They would ask for "Baksheesh Sob", meaning either money or food.

Arriving at the town of Rawalpindi we boarded an Indian bus. Our luggage was thrown into a luggage rack on top of the bus. We were driven up the mountain to the rest camp that was located just a few miles from Murree. The route was extremely dangerous.

Half way to the rest camp the road was barricaded. The road was so narrow that traffic was closed for an hour to allow one-way traffic down the mountain. At the end of an hour our procession proceeded upward. The road became so narrow that at times we had to backup to the very edge of the cliff before the driver could negotiate the turn. A rock "Wallia" sat beside the driver and he had a pile of rocks next to him on the floor. I wondered why he had those rocks and I soon found out. When the driver had to back up to the cliff in order to make a curve the rock Wallia's job was to leap out of the bus and place a rock under our back wheels to prevent us from going over the cliff. On one particular curve the turn was sharp the driver had to back up three times in order to get around it. Those of us who were seated in the back row found ourselves hanging out over the edge of the cliff. At the rest camp we referred to those turns as rock one, rock two and so forth.

Our rest camp stay was very relaxing. There were no duties. We played tennis, hiked and/or rode old horses around the mountain. The horses had little fear of heights. They would walk you along the very edge of the cliff. Many times you could look down a sheer cliff several thousand feet. The apprehension of falling never left me as we wound the mountain.

Receiving supplies was a real problem in the CBI theater. We were at the very end of the US supply lines. When the Chinese began their advance into the Kaolin Mountain area of Burma supplies became a real problem. At times, both the Chinese and their American advisers were forced to live on bamboo shoots and what Burmese livestock they could find. The troops were reduced to near starvation.

The worst of this supply failure was around Chaikung, where the Japs were besieged. When the Chinese captured the pillboxes, they wondered why they only found 75 Japs. They knew at least 300 Japs had opposed them. They obtained the answer when they inspected the Jap kitchen. The Japs had been eating one another after running out of rations.

On most occasions, the Japs would slay their wounded when forced to retreat.

The Chinese placed little value on the lives of their men. A commander could execute a soldier but he had to get special orders from his group to kill a muse or a horse.

Supplies to China had to be flown over the Himalayas, (the Hump). The mountains were littered with the remains of American airplanes. The area was known as the aluminum trail because of airplanes that crashed trying to fly over the Hump.

The Himalaya range was a thing of terror. No person in his or her right mind would want to fly over the Hump. There were green tangled jungles, snakes, wild animals and savage native headhunters. There were twisting mountain gorges over 30,000 feet. Terrifying storms raged through lizard back passes. Winds of more than 100 miles per hour blasted up and down drafts that tossed a plane like a matchstick. A plane could suddenly be tossed a thousand feet up or dropped like a rock thousands of feet onto the rocks or jungle below.

Flying the Hump, you could encounter pouring, drenching rain, or sleet and ice that could tear the wings off your plane. There were howling snow storms with mist and fog and thick black clouds and roaring thunder storms. Diving Jap fighter planes combined with roving Jap patrols that captured or killed crashed American airmen.

The 14th Air Force dropped ammunition, rice and raincoats; but flying had to be stopped because of wet weather. More than 150 coolie supply porters fell to their death on the precipitous monsoon-muddy trails.

There were thousands of square miles of clogging, choking vegetation, making it impossible for two parachuted airmen, only fifty feet apart, to hear each other when they shouted.

Airmen shot down or forced to crash land, if they were lucky, would hack their way through the thick jungle or climb desperately up over the craggy mountains to get back to an air base. The trip back could take them a week or up to three months. They made it out alive if Japs, or hunger, or headhunters didn't kill them.

Hacking their way out of the jungle was a terrible experience. You were usually soaking wet and sleeping was almost impossible because of animals and mosquitoes. Giant bloodsucking leeches dropped from trees and stuck to your face. Necks and arms were soon covered. Within hours your wrists and ankles would be swollen and your body shook with cold and fever.

There were wild elephants and charging water buffaloes to contend with. Bengal tigers were common. The Nagas, of the Naga Hills, were known for their headhunting. They took only the heads from their enemies. They were, for the most part, hospitable to the Americans. One of their practices was that of using tadpoles as the chief ingredient in the main dish of a Naga feast. They would dump several buckets of live tadpoles into boiling water for Naga stew. Tadpoles as used by the Nagas were "jungle lobsters".

Of course, not all natives were friendly to the Americans. The Lisus, in northern Burma, were so belligerent they set loaded crossbows on trails near their village. Arrows were poisoned and pointed against all comers. The Lolos, in West Yunnan, disposed of their dead in baskets hung from trees. They were uncommunicative people. They were generally unfriendly and feared because they practiced slavery.

The jungle of Burma was the most forbidding in the world and had the world's worst climate. Monsoons began in May and ran through October. Between 200 and 800 inches of rain fell during this period of time. During the monsoon, it could rain up to 16 inches a day. Creeks turned into rivers and those rivers rose as much as 25 feet a day. Men got jungle rot from wearing boots. Swarms of flies always came in after the rains and would drive you crazy.

Everywhere there were bloodsucking leeches by the thousand moving toward you like measuring worms in the trees, bushes, grass, and ground. Dropping off low branches they would fasten themselves to you and work their way to your arms and legs. Sometimes you wouldn't feel the bite until you saw blood streaming down your arms and legs, because they injected some sort of anesthetic as well as an anticoagulant to keep the blood flowing. We used rock salt and cigarettes were to remove the leeches. If you pulled the leech off, its head would remain in you, making an ugly sore. If the sore remained untreated, it would rot the flesh to the bone.

Troops in Burma were up against one of the worst terrains in the world. They had to wade in mud up to their knees, climb jagged mountains, cut their way through thick jungle and cross rivers on rafts that sometimes were swept six to eight miles downstream. They had to hack their way through razorback elephant grass as high as six feet.

The jungles were so thick everyone was forced to stay on trails. You never knew when you would run into an ambush by the Japs. The terror some men went through left an indelible mark on many. Some men became nutty as the proverbial fruitcake.

Americans captured by the Japs were usually tortured. Many had their heads, hands, and feet cut off. The Japs would mount the head on a pole for all to see, it was their way of warning Americans what their fate would be if captured.

The Hooghly River runs for about 125 miles between the Bay of Bengal and Calcutta. Near Calcutta it flows past palm trees, which partially conceal temples and decaying palaces.

Along its banks are the world's worst slums. There are also crocodiles there as well as leopards. Sometimes humans were snatched. Women lined the shore washing their clothing, slapping clothes up and sown against the stone steps of the gates.

There was death there as well as life. Bodies were cremated daily on the steps like those on a bonfire of logs. Flutes would be blown before they were scattered into the river. But sometimes a man would die and his family would not have enough money for his burning. So they quietly slipped him into the Hooghly. A day or two later, on some mud flat a mile downstream, dogs would be chewing over a floppy seemingly rubberized thing. By some mysterious chemistry it would be bleached almost white from head to foot.

In 1943 a disastrous famine struck India. The sidewalks of the cities became home for thousands of villagers who flocked there in a desperate bid to survive. They lived, slept, bathed, and died there. Each morning the streets and sidewalks were searched for dead bodies. Surviving mothers begged us for their children whose weakened bodies clearly showed that death was just around the corner. People searched garbage cans for scraps of food. (I previously alluded to this problem.) It was estimated that 11,000 people died weekly just in the province of Bengal. The famine was throughout India.

Chapter Seven

BACK TO THE U.S.A.

By November 15, 1944 I had accumulated enough points for rotation to the States. We could return by plane or ship, I chose flying.

We boarded a C-54 transport at Karachi Air Base. We flew northwest over the Arabian Sea and the Persian Gulf and we landed somewhere in Arabia for our first refueling. After taking off we flew past the Dead Sea. The pilot pointed out Bethlehem to us. He flew very low to give us a good view. I feasted my eyes on this Holy City until it disappeared from view.

We flew over the Suez Canal on our trip to Cairo. Approaching the airfield we banked low over the pyramids and Sphinx. After landing we walked to the hangar to refresh ourselves. We walked past several wrecked German planes. A huge Nazi symbol had been painted on the side of the hangar. It had been partially painted over by the Americans. There were many holes made by machine gun fire in the side of the hangar. Apparently heavy fighting had taken place here.

Leaving Cairo we proceeded westward. Suddenly one of our engines caught on fire. The flames were blowing past my window. The situation was critical. The pilot feathered the prop and we limped into the Algiers airport. The British were in charge there. We were taken into town and put up for the night in a hotel run by the British. We had our first taste of English food. It wasn't bad. The next morning, our engine being repaired, we took off for Casablanca.

Arriving at Casablanca we were placed in a former prisoner of war camp. The camp once contained German and Italian prisoners. They had been relocated to other prisons. Some of the Germans had been taken to America. We were held there several days awaiting the arrival of more homeward bound troops. Eventually there were enough of us to fill a ship and we were loaded aboard the USS Grant for a fifteen-day journey to the States.

There was an extreme amount of damage in Casablanca's city and harbor. We passed several sunken ships as we steamed out of the harbor. As we passed the entrance and headed out into the Atlantic I thought of how clean it looked and smelled, compared to the places I had been the last two and one half years. The smells of India were still overpowering.

We did not encounter any real problems crossing the Atlantic. Then two days out of New York, we ran into the tail of a hurricane. The ship rocked back and forth. Men would fall trying to walk. We could hear things crashing throughout the vessel. The troops were restricted below deck. Tremendous waves crashed against the side of the ship and rolled across the deck. For the first time in my life I was seasick.

The storm passed as we pulled into New York harbor. I actually waved at that grand old lady in the harbor as we passed her on our starboard side. Tears of relief and joy ran down our faces. All the built up tension and emotions drained away and in their place was a sense of serenity. I was home and safe. The feeling was exhilarating. I wanted to shout, "Hey look at me, America! I'm home!" I had made it back.

We disembarked and fell into ranks on the pier. Red Cross workers gave each of us a cup of coffee and a doughnut. It was December 15, 1944. We boarded a train for Camp Kilmer, New Jersey, a processing center. We were reprocessed and I received orders to proceed to Santa Ana, California. I was given a twenty-one day delay in route.

I used the delay in route to visit my family in Elkhart,

Indiana. I arrived home just two days before Christmas. This was my first visit home since joining the Army. We had a lot of catching up to do. It was a joyous occasion. Most of my friends were in the service, nevertheless it was wonderful talking to old friends. In the United States there was very little news concerning the CBI Theater of operations. I never understood the fact that so few in this country knew of the efforts of those who served in the CBI. The South Pacific and the European theaters were making headlines. *We were in the forgotten theater.*

When my leave was over I took a train to California. The thing I remember the most about the Santa Ana Redistribution Center was the food. Many American airmen from overseas passed through Santa Ana for reassignment. We were treated like heroes. The food was terrific. Tables were loaded with everything imaginable. You could have all you wanted to eat. I had not seen that much good food since entering the service. In the CBI Theater we had little more than Spam every day to eat.

During my interview for reassignment the man asked if I still wanted to attend the Aviation Cadet School. My answer was no. I had seen too many pilots maimed and killed overseas. I was sick and tired of all that, I yearned for a little peace and quiet.

I was assigned to the Will Rogers Air Force Base in Oklahoma City. Upon my arrival I discovered they had no idea just what to do with me. Finally two other fellows and I were assigned to dismantling a B-24 that had crashed. It was a boring job. When I went to the mess hall for the first time I noticed German prisoners of war pulling KP duties. I remained at Will Rogers for several months before being transferred to the Coffeyville Air Base in Kansas.

I was assigned to the 489th Photo Reconnaissance Unit. I

worked on the P-38 Lightening. It was a beautiful plane, a long-range single seat escort fighter. It had two 1425 horse-powered Allison engines. Its maximum speed was 411 miles per hour at 25,000 feet. It could cruise at 290 miles per hour. Its range on internal fuel was around 475 miles. The P-38 was 37 feet long. It had one 20-millimeter cannon and four 0.50 inch machine guns, and could carry up to a 3,200 pound bomb.

I enjoyed working on the P-38. Usually two or three of us worked on each plane. Overseas each crew chief worked on two planes. Of course overseas we were always short of help. The two Allison engines were the same type I had worked on before. Therefore, I had little trouble converting my expertise to another plane.

One afternoon, while sitting in the dentist chair, I was ap-proached by a soldier. He handed me my traveling orders. I was to leave for Camp Atterbury, Indiana and from there I was to go to the Army Air Force Base at Baer Field, Fort Wayne, Indiana. The war was over and I was to be discharged.

At Baer Field my records were brought up to date and I received medals I had earned.

I was discharged on October 24, 1945. I had been in the military service for three years, six months, twenty-three days and seventeen minutes.

~ ~ ~ ~

AFTERTHOUGHTS

VIEWS OF INDIA AND WAR IN THE CBI

Arriving in Karachi was awesome for us young Americans. Most of us had never been over a hundred miles from our home before entering the service. Now we found ourselves thousands of miles from the old USA on the other side of the world.

We realized mother India had cradled civilization for over five thousand years. With her population of over 400,000,000 she was the goal of the Axis during the war. Warlords of the Japanese Empire expected to join forces with the Germans under Hitler, in their blueprint of world conquest.

It was 1942. While the British were trying to hold their defense lines in India, the Americans were on the way. At the time of our arrival in India, the American Flying Tigers, under General Chennault in China, were creating havoc among the Japanese. In addition to the American and British troops in India there were around 2,000,000 Indian volunteer troops.

In order for the Japanese to succeed in their plan to conquer Asia, they planned to thrust through Burma into India. They would drive across India to a planned junction with the Germans, who only in 1942 gave any indication of smashing through Egypt and joining their Asiatic partner in Iran or Afghanistan.

In 1942 the Japanese launched a four-pronged drive into India from Burma. They tried to capture Imphal and the Bengal Assam railroad line. Another column swept toward Silchar, an important railway town west of Imphal. The enemy crossed into India for the first time in March 1944. They infiltrated into Imphal and Kohima. That was as far as they got.

Fighting was furious. The last Jap was thrown out of India in August. The American public was never told of the Japanese retaliation against the Chinese because of this action. They sent 53 battalions of infantry raging through Chekiang. They annihilated entire villages suspected of having aided Doolittle's fliers. The Japanese killed 250,000 Chinese and plowed up every airfield in an area of 29,000 square miles.

The Japanese would strip captured Americans, tie them to trees and use them for bayonet practice. They soaked captured ambulances with gasoline and set them on fire, wounded soldiers and all.

Death in India was an everyday occurrence. No place on earth was death treated so insignificantly during World War II. Death blanketed the cities like a silent fog. Death was the unseen presence that walked beside every GI. There was death in the streets by starvation. Death by cholera and rat-borne plague. Death in alleys in unattended childbirth. There were deaths in the slums from rampant untreated disease. Death in temples and mosques in religious riots. Death at the hands of the Indian police breaking up demonstrations against the British rule. Death came in violent spasms to rickshaw pullers and others by opium and bhang. Death was an epidemic.

Death was so commonplace and contemptible; the street crews who collected garbage also piled the street dead into their carts and wagons. Sometimes the corpse crews had to drive away the snarling jackals and wild dogs. We Americans were outraged at the callus and cavalier attitude of the Indian Police toward their own.

At Karachi Airfield Base, where I had pulled many hours of guard duty, there was a giant hanger that had been built to accommodate the ill-fated R-100, a British dirigible that had crashed in France at the start of its planned flight to India.

Troops were permitted to visit Karachi when they were not

on duty. The main section of Karachi was fairly clean. There was unbelievable squalor and poverty in areas surrounding the downtown area, which was off-limits to military personnel. Visiting the city was usually an unpleasant experience. Beggars of all ages, shapes and description would besiege you. Most were dirty and many were horribly deformed and so grotesque that revulsion overcame our pity. It was said that parents often maimed their children to prepare them for begging

There was no food served on the trains in India. There were no modern toilet facilities. The train stopped at a number of small towns in route where you could get food and personal niceties. Many natives did not use toilet paper but washed their private parts with water. You would see them doing this in all parts of India.

Drinking water, not in the camp liter bag, was kept in unglazed jugs in your bay area. Slight evaporation through the jug walls kept the water cool. In the hot summer months we would sweat under a tour mosquito net that was tucked under our mattress. The next night we would sleep in sweat of the night before. It took a long time for things to dry out.

Your food was really an experience because of little or no refrigeration available. It consisted of non-perishables, powdered eggs, potatoes, milk, canned Spam and corned beef. The flour was infested with local insects. When we were served bread we tried to remove those insects. Later on we paid no attention but just ate them along with our meal.

During my years in India I found the meals they created made a most rigid diet. Everyone who served there left much trimmer than when they arrived. For example, a friend of mine weighed 180 pounds when he arrived in India. When the man left he weighed 135 pounds. The only fat people were visiting generals. Breakfast usually consisted of fried Spam, canned vegetables, and coffee. On Sundays cakes would be baked out of that buggy flour.

General Chennault's planes operated at the end of the world's longest supply lines. It was 12,000 miles from the US to Bombay, India. It took two months for a cargo ship to travel that distance. Upon arriving in India, supplies had to cross India by rail for 1,500 miles and be transferred to an ancient railway between Assam and Bengal. The Americans called it the "Toonerville Trolley". The railway changed gage three times. Its freight had to cross the un-bridged Brahamputra, one of India's great rivers, by barge. Arriving in Assam, the Air Force Transport Command flew the supplies across the "Hump" to Kunming, China.

Flying supplies to China was a mind-boggling logistical problem. General Chennault once said, "It was as though an air force based in Kansas was supplied from San Francisco to bomb targets from Maine to Florida." In order to drop one ton of bombs on Japanese held Shanghai, 18 tons of supplies had to be delivered to an Indian port in support of that operation.

When Colonel Jimmy Doolittle led a flight of B-25's off an aircraft carrier on April 16, 1942, the American public hailed this first attack against the Japanese mainland as a wonderful accomplishment. After striking Tokyo, the planes flew on the China. Many crashed landed in Chekiang province.

Landhi Field lay about fifteen miles from Karachi. The country was rather flat and dry. It lay on the edge of the Sind Desert. The field was comprised of a group of widely separated, low flat buildings on a sun-baked expanse of sand. The airfield with a control tower and an alert shack, Crew Chief Shack, was about half a mile away from our barracks.

Landhi was chosen for a very sound training program. Fighter pilots from China and Burma, who had completed their combat missions, would spend about six weeks there on their way home. They would pass on their hard won experiences to the replacement pilots who were heading for combat. New pilots were exposed to the most up-to-date tactics and techniques. The system worked very well. Most of our planes were war weary P-40's that had been in Africa and China before coming to Landhi Field. We also had some P-51s along with a few P-47s.

At Landhi, pilots were introduced to paraphrase antipersonnel weapons. Each bomb weighed about sixty pounds and consisted of a cast coil spring, filled with explosive and a small parachute on one end and a long striker at the other end. The parachute stopped the bombs forward movement on release and dropped rapidly, exploding about one foot above the ground. The spring would break into small fragments that blasted with tremendous velocity over a circular area of several hundred feet. A P-40 would carry three paraphrases under each wing.

The area around Karachi and Landhi Field from the air had a stark beauty with the Sind Desert stretching to the north and east with miles of deserted beaches along the Arabian Sea. It was the ideal spot for combat training with many deserted areas bombing and gunnery practice. We introduced *shadow gunnery* at Landhi. An airplane would fly at about 1,000 feet over the deserted beach area, so that its shadow ran along the sand. Other fighters would take turns diving and shooting at the shadow.

The crew chiefs responsibility was to strap on the pilots chute and safety belt and then plug in their helmet radio leads and throat mike. When the pilot was secure, we would yell "clear" and he would start his engine.

Being a member of the ground crew as a crew chief, airplane and engine mechanic, I had certain daily responsibilities. Rising before dawn every day to make ready the plane before the morning mission. We would perform our arduous tasks late into the evening, under the scorching sun and stifling heat of the evening.

Planes were refueled between each flight. Armor personnel clambered on and under the hot wings. They manhandled the heavy bombs and ammunition belts and they changed gun barrels when necessary. The guns were cleaned and lubricated.

We crew chiefs lived through our pilots. We were thrilled every time a mission was successful. We suffered when our plane was damaged or the pilot was lost. Overjoyed if he turned up safe. We received few promotions that side of the ocean and few medals, but I believe our dedication to our pilots and the overall cause was unequaled.

A well-worn camel trail from Karachi to Hyderabad ran by Landhi's main gate. Six or eight caravans on camels would plod along this trail every night, loaded with trade goods. The lead camel wore a large bell hanging from its neck. The camel drivers were invariable lulled to sleep by the rhythm of the bell. We too would fall asleep with the gentle sound of the bells and the crying of the jackals in our ears.

The Sind Desert, where I was stationed, was hot and the winds were like a blast from an oven. On occasion there was flying sand. Sand would cover everything, your clothing, food, bunks, etc. If you slapped your hand on you bunk the sand and dust rose in a cloud. In this hot humid weather leather turned green overnight from mildew. Your shoes needed cleaning every morning.

— — —

I have written about the trains we took to the Himalayan rest camp, but I would like to describe them in possibly more detail. Indians usually hung all over the outside of the cars.

The cars we rode in were like wooden boxcars. Hard wooden benches on each side and a wider bench running lengthwise through the center. In one corner there was a toilet cubicle about four feet square with a door. The entire floor was sloped toward the center, where there was a hole. You could see the railroad ties through that hole. On each side of the hole was concrete padding about two inches high in the shape of a human foot. There was a handle on the wall to hold on to while you relieved yourself. There was no toilet paper.

In the Burmese jungles there were dumdum flies whose bites produced fierce itching and tiny buffalo flies that passed through your mosquito netting, bitting all night.

— — —

I've mentioned the leeches in my previous remarks but feel they deserve more attention. There was the three-inch common leech, the three inch buffalo leech, and the monster elephant leech that grew to nearly a foot in length. If you had to spend time in the jungle you would soon be oozing in blood from leech bites. Animals suffered even more. Donkeys, for example, had their fetlocks running with blood and crawling with maggots that hatched in their open wounds.

— — —

When the Japanese tried to invade India through the Imphal plains and the town of Kohima, they were repulsed after many furious battles. The valor of the Japanese soldier was extraordinary. They were awarded medals for campaigns and long service. None was given for bravery, bravery was simply assumed. They were trained in Bushide. They were instructed to choose death over captivity. In desperate situations the Japanese soldier would save their last grenade or bullet for themselves. If four hundred Japanese were ordered to hold a position you had to kill three-hundred ninety-five before it was ours. The last five would kill themselves.

In the battles of Imphal and Kohima the Japanese suffered the greatest defeat in their history. All together they lost 30,000 killed and 25,000 sick or wounded. Their 25th Army was no longer a fighting force.

Four months after their attempt to enter India, General Mutaguchi's defeated army began their withdrawal through the Burma jungles. The troops were exhausted and emaciated. They were barefoot and ragged. They threw away everything except canes to help them walk. They had nothing to eat except grass and water. British troops following the retreating Japanese came upon unburied corpses by the hundreds, scores of wounded, and land strewn with the bodies of men shot by their comrades to spare them the disgrace of capture.

— — —

For a great many CBI veterans the most meaningful part of our lives was spent in the Orient in World War II. We were giving of ourselves for our country. We like to feel that hidden under our desire for achievement, there is a noble and patriotic side of our nature that never dies.

CBI history tells us thousands of Americans sacrificed much in the Far East. Many lost their lives repelling the Japanese invaders. We are told we were badly outnumbered by the enemy and that we had great difficulties because our regular supply lines were so badly stretched three fourths of the way around the world. I do not readily recall the history or statistics. I only remember that part of the war that touched me personally, physically, or emotionally. I remember my fears and my elation when these fears were overcome.

I recall the most famous monument possible of the whole war, the Naga Memorial dedicated to the heroes of the battle of Kohima. It stands outside the entrance to their cemetery.

This large piece of rough stone, dragged up the hill from a local quarry, is as striking in its simplicity as is the evocative inscription:

> *When You Go Home*
> *Tell Them About Us*
> *For Your Tomorrow*
> *We Gave Our Today*

AFTERTHOUGHTS

MY RETURN TO THE USA FROM INDIA

The fifteen-day trip from Casablanca, Africa to the USA was uneventful until we hit the tail end of a hurricane two days out of New York harbor. The ship rolled and tossed. The bow would plunge into the angry sea, then rise high out of the water only to smash down again. Everything on board was jarred. Thirty to forty-foot waves crashed repeatedly on the deck with thunderous roars. Rolling across the deck, they would smash into the bulkheads and anything in their path was in peril. Items not secured were swept overboard.

Men moaned "Let me die." Few of us escaped being seasick. I was one of those who thought he was going to die. I wanted to relieve myself of the terrible sickness. I had volunteered for fireguard so I could receive three meals a day. I became sick around midnight while on guard duty. I rushed to the latrine and vomited until nothing but dry heaves were left. Returning to my post, I was unable to maintain my balance on the rolling deck. I was dizzy and tossed from one wall to another. I lay down in a hammock while the world spun around me. A lieutenant shook me by the arm arousing me from my slumber. He asked if I was on guard duty. I explained my situation and he said for me to go to my quarters and get some sleep, he would finish my watch. The next morning the sun came out and the sea had calmed. The wind receded and by noon I was feeling fine again.

The change in the climate wrought havoc among the troops. We were not prepared for the cruel December winter weather. We shivered in our thin khaki uniforms. I yearned for the warmth of India.

The water in the New York harbor was calm as we passed The Statue of Liberty. Our ship pulled up beside a dock and the gangplank was lowered. We disembarked and stood in rank on the pier.

It was the first time I had stepped on American soil in over two and a half years. Words cannot describe the feeling that passed over me.

There were no bands to greet us. No parades or speeches. A few Red Cross ladies met us and distributed coffee and donuts. I will never forget those ladies. They braved that cold winter morning just to greet us. I've often wondered if they knew just how much we appreciated their being there.

What Great Memories

Many years have passed since the early forty's but I still remember:

- The smell of the old P-40

- The rising, whining crescendo of the inertia started, just before engaging.

- The sudden straining "whine down" of the engagement.

- The unavoidable coughing and stuttering spits of the Allison engine.

- In a final gasp, the surging chugging caught as the 12 cylinders gained RPM. They would erase away their starting smoke, aided by the blast from the whirling prop.

- The whistling of the winding down of the prop, after the clatter and noise of the engine ceased.

- The rolling sound of the canopy, my greeting my returning pilot as he rolled it back, exposing the cockpit smells of hydraulic and petroleum fluid. This mixed with the aroma of burnt 100 octane gasoline.

- The roaring of your planes swift departure, then the marked absence of sound. The landing strip would remain silent until their return.

AFTERTHOUGHTS

Remembrances of Childhood
in Elkhart, Indiana

Growing up on the banks of the St. Joseph River.

We lived across the river from McNaughton Park. During spring rains much of the park would be flooded. As a youth I, along with other children, would swim across the river to the park. On many warm days we would jump or dive off the old Iron Bridge leading to the park on Bridge Street. The bridge was a popular meeting place. We would climb over the hand railing and jump or dive into the river. More adventurous souls would climb the iron support rails to the very top and from there dive into the river. Children no longer use that as a swimming hole.

At the park's west end, where the soap-box derby hill used to be, was a small bayou surrounded by tall weeds. We boys would row our boat into this bayou to catch frogs and turtles by hand. Turtles were used for racing and later returned to the river. The frogs were used for jumping contests and for fishing.

West of the present pavilion was a small pond. During the winter months it would freeze over and we would ice skate there. In those days skates were clamped onto your shoes. Usually they would fall off several times before you finished skating.

Churches held revival meetings in the park. We lived just across the river from there, and we could hear the organ and the folks singing. On Easter Sunday there were egg hunts and we would keep busy running from bush to tree, etc. looking for those eggs.

Golden Glove boxing matches were held in the park and they usually drew a large crowd. The entertainment in the park during the summer months was usually free. However, when the Clyde Beatty circus came to town or when the carnival arrived, there was a charge for those things.

My father and I set traps along the river in the winter. We caught muskrats and mink. We skinned and stretched their hides on racks made from wood or wire. In the spring the hides were sold to a fur dealer.

During the summer months we trapped turtles with traps made of chicken wire. We knew when there was a turtle in the trap, we could see ripples coming from the trap top. The meat from those turtles was sold to be eaten by our friends. Mother was very good at preparing turtle meat for the evening meal. This took place during the great depression and a person was not fussy about what he ate. There was little money to go around and a person did just about anything to get food on the table.

One evening while running our traps I saw a stump just ahead of the boat. I told Dad about it and he said, "You don't need me to tell you about stumps as I know every stump in this river." At that juncture the boat slid upon the stump. Dad said very nonchalantly, "That's a new one."

Turtle Bill (William Maynard) lived on a small island at Mosquito Glen. This area is now known as Treasure Island. Bill was a true river rat. He trapped and hunted along the river, similar to Dad. Bill would drag the river for clams.

Some weekends clambakes were held. There was demand for their shells by the button factories. Clamshells were thrown into piles and then loaded onto trucks for transportation to the factories. While cleaning clams you would, on occasion, find fresh water pearls. My mother had a large jar full of these pearls. It was my understanding they had little commercial value.

The clam drag was placed on the stern of the boat and lowered into the water. It would be dragged for a short distance. Then Bill would pull it into the boat removing anything caught on the hooks. I recall Bill recovering several bodies; people who had drowned and the police were unable to recover them. He used his drag in that operation.

I fished a great deal in those days. My father built a smokehouse and would smoke the larger fish. The best place to fish was at the rubbish piles. A tree or large branch would fall into the river and floating material would catch on the branches forming a rubbish pile. We boys had names for those piles; the little rubbish pile, the big rubbish pile, etc.

On West Franklin Street, across from Krau Street, there was a small grocery store. The people in the neighborhood purchased their goods there. Behind the store was a boathouse. My friends built a clubhouse in the loft and we spent many idle hours there. During the warm summer months we watched Boy Scouts cruising down the river in their canoes. Young lovers in their canoes would float the river. Some fellows would play banjos for their girl friends. It seemed a wonderful way to cruise the river.

My brother Jack and his friends built a platform on the top of our high riverbank. From this platform, we would swing out over the river and drop with a splash into the deeper water. One day while swimming at our favorite swimming hole on Edgewater Drive, a young man drove a car to the river's edge. He yelled for us to look out as he raced his car toward the riverbank. At the last minute he jumped from the car as it shot out and over the bank into the river. We watched it slowly sink from view. I never did understand why he did that. Years later I was still losing fish line on the wreck.

We built a small hut on an island new Mosquito Glen. We

would camp there on occasions. One evening while lying near an open fire, my pants caught on fire. I still carry a scar on my leg after all these years.

I used to row our boat up stream to Grady's Dairy. It was located near Bridge Street on Franklin Street. I would purchase a gallon of skim milk for ten cents. It was always cold and tasted so good on a hot summer day.

There were few ducks or geese on the river in those days. I'm afraid they would not have lasted long. People had a hard time making ends meet and a fowl dinner was a meal fit for a king. There were, however, many sea gulls. There were few boats of any kind on the lower St. Joseph River. Most boats were manually operated.

There was dancing on Saturday night at "Cocky Stanford's" by the dam on Johnson Street. My mother ran the kitchen. We children would eat there and watch the square and round dancing. Everyone seemed to have a good time. I recall floating down the river and picking elderberries along its bank for my father to make wine. Picking wild strawberries in the summer along the river was a favorite pastime.

Winters seemed much colder than now. Perhaps it was because we did not have the warm clothing we have now. I remember, after a big snowstorm, the horse plows plowing the sidewalks in the city. We would walk to school in the tracks of autos.

— The End —

CPSIA information can be obtained at www.ICGtesting.com
Printed in the USA
LVOW131845060113

314510LV00002B/143/P

9 781611 701043